Think Beyond

OrangeBooks Publication

1st Floor, Rajhans Arcade, Mall Road, Kohka, Bhilai, Chhattisgarh 490020
Website: **www.orangebooks.in**

First Edition, 2025

ISBN: 978-93-7426-353-2

THINK BEYOND

BALANCING LOGIC, INSTINCT, AND INTENT

RISHABH CHOURE

OrangeBooks Publication
www.orangebooks.in

Dedication

To my mother and father,

whose quiet sacrifices, whispered lessons,

and unwavering love built the foundation of this work.

And to every seeker standing at the edge of reason,

Looking beyond the obvious — this is for you.

Foreword

A Personal Note

"Before I share the perspectives in this book, I want to honour the people who made this journey possible. To my mother and Late father: thank you for your support and your intent, which have quietly guided me throughout. Without you, these words would not exist." This book isn't written to give you answers. It's written to provoke questions — the kind that sit quietly at the back of your mind and demand honesty. We live in a world obsessed with speed, but clarity takes pausing, reflecting, and sometimes even unlearning. That's what this book asks of you: to pause and to Think Beyond.

Contents

Part I – Logic

Chapter - One
Understanding Logic

Every day, we face choices—some tiny, like whether to eat aloo paratha or oats for breakfast, and others huge, like whether to change careers, move cities, or marry someone. In both cases, something guides us. Sometimes it's instinct, sometimes it's blind habit, and sometimes it's logic. Out of these, logic is the most reliable compass we have—if we know how to use it.

But let's be honest: logic isn't glamorous. Nobody writes love songs about logic. Instagram reels aren't going viral with hashtags like #LogicalLiving. People don't quote Descartes in their wedding vows. Yet, quietly, behind the scenes, logic is what helps us and not mess up our lives completely.

Think about it. You don't need logic to choose between samosa and kachori—your taste buds and cholesterol levels will fight that battle for you. But when the decision carries weight—career, relationships, money—logic steps up. It's the sober friend at the party who reminds you not to text your ex at 2 a.m.

Why Logic Matters

Logic matters because it creates a filter between chaos and clarity. Without it, life is basically Twitter—loud, emotional, often wrong, and full of people shouting opinions. With logic, you get to pause, weigh, analyse, and ask: Does this make sense?

- **Clarity in Chaos Imagine losing your job suddenly. Instinct says:** panic. Emotion says: cry into a pillow. Logic says: "Okay, let's list savings, calculate expenses, and plan next steps." Which one actually gets you through the storm? Not the pillow.
- Decision-Making in Real Life A friend once asked me if she should leave her stable bank job to start a bakery. Her parents said no, her heart said yes, and her logic… well, it was confused. We sat down and made a simple sheet: savings, potential rent, number of cakes needed to break even. By the end, she saw the risks clearly but also the possibility. That's the power of logic—it doesn't kill dreams, it makes them practical.
- **Defence Against Manipulation Let's face it:** advertisers, politicians, and even relatives with too many WhatsApp forwards are constantly trying to manipulate us. Logic is armour. It asks, "Who benefits if I believe this?" Or does the evidence back this claim?

A Personal Story

"I have always been curious, asking 'why' before accepting anything at face value. This search for clarity has shaped the way I think and learn." "Why do we solve it this way?" "Why can't the Earth be flat if it feels flat when I walk?" (Don't worry, I didn't join the flat-earthers). I wanted reasons for everything.

That curiosity turned into overthinking. If I had to buy a phone, I would compare twenty models, check RAM, camera, battery life, and even how many reviews mentioned "heating issue." But when it came to life's biggest questions—like what career to choose—people around me were shockingly casual. "Beta, engineering kar lo. Safe hai." That's not logic. That's copy-paste tradition disguised as advice.

Logic, when I finally started using it properly, became a tool of liberation. It allowed me to see that "safe" often meant "miserable but socially approved."

Case in Point: The Logic of "Why"

I had a relative who swore engineering was the only real career. According to him, medicine was second-best, but writing? Music? Sports? "Beta, that's just a hobby. Not a future."

His reasoning? Simple: Sharmaji's son did engineering. Now he earns in lakhs. Case closed.

But here's the thing: one data point is not logic—it's laziness. Logic demands you ask: Why did Sharmaji's son succeed? Was it the degree, his passion, his timing, or sheer luck? If another Sharmaji's son failed with the same degree, does that mean the degree itself was flawed? Of course not. Logic doesn't cherry-pick; it considers patterns, not isolated examples.

Logic in Everyday Life

We often treat logic like an elite skill reserved for scientists or philosophers. But the truth is, it applies everywhere:

- **In shopping:** Advertisers push "limited - time offers."
- **Logic asks:** "Is it actually a deal, or did they just mark it up first?"
- **In friendships:** Someone constantly takes from you but rarely gives.
- **Logic whispers:** "This is not friendship, this is freeloading."
- **In health:** A friend swears by a miracle diet.
- **Logic says:** "If it worked, wouldn't doctors recommend it?"

The problem isn't that we don't have logic—it's that we don't always listen to it.

The Missed Opportunity

Let me tell you about a guy who had two job offers. He made spreadsheets, weighed pros and cons, called ten friends, even flipped a coin (and then analysed why the coin landed that way). By the time he decided, both offers had expired.

That's the dark side of logic: when it turns into paralysis. Logic should be a compass, not a jail cell. Thinking endlessly is not the same as deciding.

How Logic Actually Works

At its core, logic is about three things:

1. Premises — the starting points. (e.g., "All humans are mortal.")
2. Reasoning — connecting the dots. (e.g., "Socrates is human; therefore Socrates is mortal.")
3. Conclusion — the result you can defend.

Sounds boring? Maybe. But this structure saves us from chaos. Without it, we're just throwing darts blindfolded.

Logic and Emotions

Here's the truth nobody tells you: logic doesn't cancel emotion—it organises it. Think about falling in love. Your heart races, your brain releases dopamine, you think, "This is the one." Logic steps in and asks: "Do we actually align in values? Or is this just chemistry with a side of Netflix rom-com fantasies?"

Logic doesn't ruin the magic. It protects you from heartbreak disguised as destiny.

Logic's Blind Spots

But let's not glorify it too much. Logic has flaws. It can't measure feelings, it can't predict human irrationality, and it often oversimplifies messy reality. You can't calculate your way out of grief. You can't spreadsheet your way into happiness.

That's why this book doesn't stop at logic. Logic is the compass—but you still need instinct to feel the path and intent to decide where you're even going.

Pause and Reflect

- Think of your last three big decisions. Which ones were guided by logic, and which by impulse? What were the outcomes?
- Recall a time when overthinking cost you an opportunity. What would have happened if you had set a time limit on deciding?
- List three beliefs you've accepted from society. Do they actually hold up when tested with logic?

Chapter - Two
The Rational Heart

Love. Probably the most overused word in human history. Songs, poems, reels, movies — everything screams about it. And yet, if you ask ten people to define it, you'll get ten different answers, ranging from "butterflies in the stomach" to "a lifelong contract signed in front of 500 relatives and a priest."

We like to think love is irrational, mysterious, something beyond explanation. And in many ways, it is. But here's the unpopular truth: even love quietly bows to logic, whether we like to admit it or not. You can't build a relationship on candlelight dinners and Spotify playlists alone. At some point, the question sneaks in: Does this make sense?

Attraction vs. Endurance

Let's start with a hard pill: attraction fades. No matter how symmetrical someone's jawline is, no matter how many gym selfies they post, time has its way. Endurance, on the other hand, grows from things that don't wrinkle — trust, patience, shared values.

Two friends of mine once debated what makes the "perfect partner."

- **Friend A's checklist:** beauty, salary, lifestyle, family status.
- **Friend B's list:** honesty, patience, emotional stability.

Fast-Forward Ten Years: Friend A got divorced within two years because, shocker, lifestyle doesn't replace loyalty. Friend B, meanwhile, built a steady, low-drama life with someone who actually listened instead of posing for Instagram couple goals.

Lesson? Logic quietly predicts outcomes that attraction refuses to see.

Logic as Guardian of Love

Logic in romance isn't the villain that kills passion. It's the quiet guardian. It asks:

- Will this person still respect me when circumstances change?
- Will they stay not just in my highs but also in my lows?
- Is this relationship sustainable, or is it just a Netflix plotline waiting to collapse?

Without logic, we confuse chemistry with compatibility. And chemistry, let's be honest, is like Wi-Fi — it feels strong at first, then mysteriously drops at the worst times.

The Illusion of Checklists

Modern dating has turned love into online shopping. Height, salary, skin tone, Instagram followers — swipe right, swipe left. But here's the twist: the things that make relationships last don't show up in a bio. You can't filter for empathy. You can't measure loyalty in centimetres.

I once knew a guy whose girlfriend ticked every box: tall, successful, glamorous. Perfect on paper. But paper burns quickly. Within two years, the fights were about everything — who controlled the money, whose friends mattered more, whose career took priority. The "perfect" checklist had no item called "respect," and that omission was fatal.

Logic, unlike checklists, asks deeper questions: Does this person share my values? Do we fight fair? Can we disagree without destroying each other?

Love Without Logic: Disaster in Slow Motion

Picture this: a couple deeply in love. They marry within six months. No conversations about money, children, or even where they want to live. Just vibes. Fast forward three years: constant arguments, resentment, therapy bills. Why? Because passion built the house, but logic forgot to check if the foundation was strong.

Logic doesn't kill love; it prevents heartbreak from predictable stupidity.

When Logic Overreaches

But let's not turn logic into a dictator. Relationships suffocate when every word, gesture, and emoji gets analysed like a court case. "She used three dots instead of one, does that mean she's angry?" or "He didn't say goodnight, maybe he's cheating." No, sometimes he just fell asleep.

Over-logic kills spontaneity. Affection needs space to breathe. Sometimes love is about letting things flow without dissecting every molecule of meaning.

Think of it this way: logic builds the frame, but emotion paints the canvas. Without the frame, the painting collapses. Without the paint, the frame is empty.

Stories From the Heart

- **The Safe Marriage:** A cousin once married a man chosen purely for "stability." He had money, status, and family approval. But no emotional connection. Within five years, she was wealthier but lonelier than ever. Logic without heart became a cage.
- **The Risky Leap:** Another friend chose a partner her family disapproved of — not rich, not from the "right" community. But logic told her: this person respects me, listens, and treats me as an equal. Ten years later, they're thriving. Sometimes, logic is about recognising values over appearances.

Science of Love and Logic

Psychologists say love has three stages: lust, attraction, and attachment. Lust runs on hormones. Attraction runs on dopamine and serotonin. But attachment — the stage that builds lifelong bonds — runs on oxytocin and trust. And trust is where logic quietly sneaks in. You can't fake reliability for decades. Logic spots the cracks early, even when lust blinds us.

Rational Red Flags

Logic is especially good at spotting red flags before emotion paints them green:

- Do they respect boundaries?
- Do they make consistent efforts, or only when it benefits them?
- Do their words align with actions?

It's not unromantic to ask these. It's survival.

Love, Logic, and Forgiveness

Logic also plays a role in forgiveness. Imagine a friend betrayed you. Logic lists reasons to cut them off: betrayal once means betrayal again, you deserve better, etc. But sometimes your heart insists forgiveness will free you. Logic says protect, heart says heal. The truth? Balance. Forgive if the person shows change, not just tears. That's logic and heart shaking hands.

Pause and Reflect

- Recall a relationship (romantic or friendship) where logic saved you from heartbreak. What signs did you notice in hindsight?
- Write down the top three qualities you'd never compromise on in a partner. Why those three?
- Think about one past relationship mistake. Was it a failure of logic, or did logic overrule emotion?
- How do you balance logic with love in your own life?

Chapter - Three

The Architecture of Society

Society is basically a giant group project we never signed up for. And like every group project, there are rules nobody fully agrees on, people who slack off, and a few who pretend to know everything but actually just copy-paste from someone else's work.

From the moment you're born, society starts shaping you. It tells you how to behave, what to believe, what jobs are "respectable," who you can love, and even how loudly you're allowed to laugh. Sounds helpful at first... until you realise half of these rules are based on tradition, fear, or just somebody's opinion that got repeated enough to become "truth."

Here's where logic enters the scene — society's silent quality check. Logic is that friend who asks, Wait, why are we even doing this? Without it, society collapses into superstition, blind obedience, and manipulation. With it, we get closer to fairness, truth, and something resembling progress.

Power and Belief

History has shown us over and over: belief is powerful. Religion, politics, ideology — they've united millions, sparked revolutions, and created art, philosophy, and culture. But the same belief systems have also divided people, justified wars, and built systems of oppression.

The difference? Intent and logic.

Belief without logic is like fire — it cooks your food, but it also burns down your house if left unchecked. When leaders twist belief for personal gain, society becomes a playground for manipulation. That's why we need logic— to separate core values from exploitative interpretations.

The Questions Logic Asks

Whenever society tells you, this is the way it's always been, logic raises its hand and asks:

- Does this belief stand up to questioning?
- Who benefits from this rule?
- Does it promote fairness or favouritism?
- If it disappeared tomorrow, would society collapse or actually improve?

Take politics, for example. It's sold as "public service." But logic asks: service for whose public? If decisions benefit donors more than citizens, maybe it's not about service at all — maybe it's about survival. Logic doesn't trust the slogan; it follows the policy.

Societal Armor

Just as logic shields individuals from fake advertisements or peer pressure, it shields societies from collapsing under dogma.

- Without logic, societies fall into cycles of blind faith.
- With logic, societies grow by re-examining traditions.

Consider education. In some communities, girls were once denied schooling because "that's just the way it is." Logic broke that chain. It asked: Does intelligence depend on gender? No. Today, millions of women thrive in professions once "forbidden."

Societies that silence logic achieve short-term obedience. But eventually, the cracks show — protests erupt, revolutions happen, structures fall apart. Societies that nurture logic may feel uncomfortable in the present but earn resilience in the future.

Culture vs. Conditioning

Let's talk about culture. Beautiful traditions like festivals, art, rituals — they give us identity. But there's a thin line between culture and conditioning.

Culture says: "We celebrate Diwali by lighting lamps."

Conditioning says: "If you don't light lamps exactly this way, you're disrespectful."

Logic protects culture by filtering out conditioning. It says: keep what uplifts, drop what oppresses.

A Personal Anecdote

I grew up hearing elders say, "Never question traditions." But I couldn't help it. Why touch elders' feet? Why fast on certain days? Why celebrate one ritual and not another? For some, the answer was genuine: respect, gratitude, mindfulness. That made sense. For others, the answer was, "Because that's how it is." That's where my brain screamed, "Not good enough."

Logic didn't make me reject tradition. It helped me separate meaning from mindless repetition.

Case Study: The Herd Instinct

Ever seen a crowd in panic? One person runs, suddenly fifty more are running, no questions asked. That's herd instinct — useful in fires, disastrous in rumours. Entire societies sometimes follow this pattern.

Take the witch trials in history. Entire communities accused women of witchcraft, burned them, and slept better at night thinking they had saved themselves. Zero evidence, just herd instinct amplified by fear. Logic would have asked: Where's the proof? Who benefits from this hysteria? But logic was duct-taped and shoved into a corner.

Modern version? Viral WhatsApp forwards. Replace witches with conspiracies, and you'll see the same herd instinct in action.

Leaders, Logic, and Lies

Society is especially vulnerable when leaders abandon logic. Charismatic speeches can make people believe anything: that an enemy is at the gate, that one community is to blame, that prosperity is just one sacrifice away. Logic is the only tool that asks: Is this leader solving problems or just creating scapegoats?

History is filled with examples — some leaders used logic to push humanity forward (abolishing slavery, granting voting rights). Others silenced it, and the results were genocides, wars, and collapsed nations.

The Fragility of Justice

Justice systems exist to keep societies balanced. But without logic, they become weapons. Think about biased laws: if punishment depends more on wealth or caste than on evidence, is it justice? Logic says no. Logic demands equality before the law, even when traditions scream otherwise.

Everyday Social Logic

Logic in society isn't just about big revolutions. It shows up in small ways, too:

- **At Work:** Promotions given to relatives over qualified candidates — logic asks: Is this meritocracy or favouritism?
- **In Families:** "Boys don't cry." Logic asks: why not? Are emotions gendered?

- **In Schools:** Forcing kids to memorise instead of understand — logic asks: are we teaching knowledge or just producing parrots?

Every small question chips away at unfair structures.

Pause and Reflect

- Think of one tradition you grew up with. Does it still hold up under logical questioning?
- Identify a social belief in your community. Who benefits from it, and who is excluded?
- How can you challenge social norms without disrespecting genuine cultural values?
- Have you ever followed a crowd without thinking? What did it cost you?

Chapter - Four
Limitations of Logic

Logic is amazing. It gives us clarity, protects us from scams, and helps us make decisions that aren't just fuelled by hormones or social pressure. But here's the twist: logic isn't invincible. It looks powerful on paper — like Superman with glasses. But even Superman has kryptonite, and logic has plenty.

We often worship logic as if it's the ultimate weapon against chaos. Yet, if you've ever frozen while making a decision, or if you've ever used logic to justify something clearly selfish, you already know: logic has holes. Big ones.

Ways Logic Falls Short

Let's break down logic's weak spots.

1. **Logic Without Evidence**

   You can have the neatest arguments in the world, but if the starting point is wrong, the conclusion is garbage. Example: "All rich people are happy. X is rich. Therefore, X is happy." Sounds neat. Totally wrong. Logic without evidence is like building a mansion on sand — looks impressive until the first storm.

2. **Logic Cannot Capture Emotion**

   Try explaining love to a logician. They'll ask for measurable metrics. But how do you quantify the comfort of someone's presence? Or the peace of forgiveness? Logic shrugs and says, "Not my department." Yet those are often the things that matter most.

3. **Logic Ignores Individuality**

   A one-size-fits-all logical solution usually fits nobody. For instance, logically, the "best" career may be the one that pays the most. But does that mean it's best for everyone? No. Logic often forgets people are messy, unique, irrational creatures.

4. **Logic Can Be Twisted by Power**

   Here's the dangerous part. Logic is easy to weaponise. Politicians, advertisers, and even friends use perfectly "logical" arguments that are designed to serve their benefit, not the truth. Example: "If you love me, you'll do this." See how sneaky that sounds?

5. **Logic Is Vulnerable to Bias**

   Ever heard of confirmation bias? It's when you only look for evidence that supports your belief. Logic should prevent this, but often it just dresses up bias in a fancy suit.

6. **Logic Oversimplifies Complexity**

   Real life isn't binary. It's not always "right or wrong," "good or bad." Logic tries to box things into categories, but human life often exists in the grey zones. Logic struggles there.

7. **Logic Without Action**

   The biggest flaw: logic alone can paralyse you. Endless calculations, infinite spreadsheets, endless "what ifs" — until the opportunity disappears. Logic without action is just mental gymnastics.

Case in Point: The Missed Train

Once, I had to catch a train. I overanalysed routes, fares, and departure times. I even calculated which platform would be less crowded. Guess what? In all that logic, I missed both trains.

That's the tragedy of over-logic: it creates the illusion of control while stealing the moment to act.

Logic vs. Heart

Imagine your friend cheated on you. Logic lists reasons not to forgive: "They'll repeat it, you deserve better, betrayal is unacceptable." But your heart whispers: "Forgiveness will set you free."

Both voices are valid. Logic protects you, but the heart heals you. Real strength lies in balancing the two. Without the heart, logic becomes a prison. Without logic, the heart becomes reckless.

The Chessboard of Life

Chess is logic's favourite metaphor. Every move calculated, consequences predicted. Perfect. But life isn't chess. In life:

- The board keeps shifting.
- The rules change mid-game.
- Sometimes, your opponent is invisible.

Logic prepares you, but it can't control the chaos. That's why people who treat life as a neat chess game often end up frustrated when real life laughs at their calculations.

Common Pitfalls and Remedies

- **Confirmation Bias**

  Remedy: Actively seek disconfirming evidence. Force yourself to read the "other side."

- **Overconfidence**

  Remedy: Invite peer review before big decisions. Let others poke holes in your logic.

- **Paralysis by Analysis**

  Remedy: Deadlines. Decide within a time limit. Favour "good enough" over "perfect."

- **Weaponised Logic**

  Remedy: Keep ethics in the mix. Logic without empathy is just manipulation.

Logic's Awkward Relationship with Instinct

Logic loves spreadsheets. Instinct loves vibes. Put them in the same room, and they fight like siblings. But the truth? Instinct often saves you when logic hesitates. Think of those moments where your gut screamed, "Don't trust this person" before any logical evidence appeared. Logic catches up later, but instinct whispers first.

Ignoring instinct because you worship logic often leaves you vulnerable. Logic isn't the enemy of instinct — it's just slower.

A Story of Overthinking

While writing this very book, I caught myself overthinking countless times. Should this idea come before that one? Should I cut this story or make it longer? Should the chapter be ten pages or twelve? I made lists, scribbled notes, rearranged paragraphs, then rearranged them again. Logic kept whispering there had to be a perfect order, a guaranteed formula. But the truth is, there wasn't. The more I chased certainty, the more I stalled. Only when I stopped trying to "solve" the book like an equation did the words finally flow. That's what overthinking does — it disguises itself as logic, but really, it's just fear in slow motion.

Why Logic Feels So Addictive

Logic gives us the illusion of safety. It feels objective, rational, and superior. That's why many people hide in logic— it feels like protection from chaos. But too much safety is also dangerous. If you never risk stepping outside the spreadsheet, you'll never discover the unknown paths life offers.

The Human Side of Logic

Let's not forget: humans invented logic. Which means it carries our flaws. Bias, ego, cultural conditioning — they sneak into even the most logical systems. That's why different cultures have different "logical" rules. Logic isn't some divine truth; it's a tool shaped by human minds.

Pause and Reflect

- Track your decisions for one week. Which ones were logical, and which were impulsive? Which worked better?
- Recall one belief you've held for years. Try to argue against it logically. Does it still hold?
- Think of one decision where logic failed you. What was missing — instinct, emotion, or timing?
- Can you identify one area where you're using logic as an excuse to delay action?

Part II – Instinct

Chapter - Five

Understanding Instinct

Instinct. Instinct. Instinct. Yes, I said it thrice — because that's how loudly it keeps knocking on our lives. You don't ask for it, you don't consciously design it, yet it shows up uninvited, whispering (sometimes screaming): Do this. Don't do that. Run. Stay. Trust. Avoid.

And the funny part? Instinct often shows up before logic even wakes up, like that one over-enthusiastic friend who arrives at the party an hour early. Logic will eventually analyse, compare, and give a verdict. But instinct doesn't wait. It reacts.

What Exactly Is Instinct?

Psychologists define instinct as unlearned, automatic behaviour — things you just do without instruction. Babies cry when they're hungry. Birds migrate without GPS. A mom somehow knows when her kid is lying, even if he swears on the family Wi-Fi.

But human instinct isn't just biological. It's also emotional, social, and deeply personal. It's the gut feeling that someone's lying. It's the unease you feel before walking down a dark alley. It's the instant connection with someone you just met.

The First Signal: Gut Feelings

Ever met a person and instantly felt, Nope, something's off? No evidence. No logic. Just vibes. Later, you find out you were right — maybe they were fake, manipulative, or hiding something. That was instinct playing detective long before logic collected the evidence.

And it works in reverse, too. You meet someone and immediately feel safe, understood, and connected. That's instinct, too. It's like your subconscious is running a background check while you're still smiling politely.

Science Behind the "Gut"

Fun fact: your gut literally has neurons — about 100 million of them. Scientists call it the "second brain." That's why stress messes with digestion and why intuition is often described as a "gut feeling." Your body isn't just being poetic — it's literally processing information outside your conscious awareness.

In short: instinct isn't magic. It's compressed experience, memory, and survival wiring. A high-speed processor your brain uses before logic even opens Excel.

Instinct in Daily Life

- **Friendships:** You might know someone for years, but deep down your gut keeps whispering, don't trust too much. Usually, it's right.

- **Relationships:** Someone may flood your inbox with "good morning, jaan" texts, but your instinct pokes you: Relax, Romeo is probably sending the same to three others. Months later, screenshots prove your gut correct.
- **Work:** Ever skipped a business deal because "something didn't feel right"? Instinct saved you from a lawsuit.

Instinct is the fast-forward button of life. Where logic takes hours, instinct takes seconds.

The Survival Angle

Instinct is ancient. Our ancestors didn't survive lions, snakes, and unpredictable weather because they had time to do a SWOT analysis. They survived because instinct said: Run.

That wiring hasn't left us. The fight-or-flight response still kicks in during modern threats — except now the "lion" might be your boss's email at 10 p.m. or your ex liking your photo after six months.

Instinct vs. Overthinking

Overthinking is instinct's enemy. Instinct says, This feels wrong. Overthinking replies: But maybe it's fine? Maybe I'm paranoid? Then, months later, you realise instinct was right all along.

We dismiss instinct because it feels unscientific. But science actually supports it. Studies show intuition is often accurate, especially in areas where you have experience. Your brain collects micro-signals you don't consciously process, then delivers the result as a "feeling."

Instinct Isn't Always Right

Here's the catch: instinct is powerful, but not flawless. Sometimes it's fear dressed as intuition. Sometimes it's bias disguised as wisdom. For example, your instinct might say, don't trust this stranger, but maybe it's just prejudice at work. That's why instinct alone can't run the show — it needs logic as backup.

Personal Story: The Warning I Ignored

Once, I had a friend whom everyone adored. Generous, funny, always smiling. But my instinct kept whispering: Be careful. I ignored it because logic listed all the positives. A year later, when trust broke, I realised instinct had seen the cracks long before my logic noticed.

When Instinct Saves You

On the flip side, instinct has saved me, too. I once turned down a quick-money investment that looked perfect on paper. No red flags logically, but my gut screamed No. A year later, the scheme collapsed, and people lost millions. Logic was fooled; instinct wasn't.

Training Instinct

The good news: instinct gets sharper with practice. The more experiences you collect, the better your subconscious gets at recognising patterns. Think of it like muscle memory. A chess master "just knows" the right move because thousands of hours are stored in his subconscious.

You can train your instinct by:

- Paying attention when it speaks.
- Reviewing past experiences to see when it was right.
- Separating genuine gut feelings from fear or bias.

Logic vs. Instinct: A Partnership

Logic and instinct aren't enemies. They're partners. Logic is the map; instinct is the traveller's hunch. Logic says, 'This is the shortest route.' Instinct says, 'Don't take that street — it feels unsafe.' The smartest decisions come when the two work together.

Why Instinct Feels Spiritual

Sometimes instinct feels bigger than us — almost spiritual. People call it "sixth sense," "divine guidance," or "the universe sending signs." Whether you see it as neurons firing or cosmic whispers, the effect is the same: a voice that speaks without words.

Pause and Reflect

- ❖ Recall a time your instinct saved you. How did it feel in the moment?
- ❖ Think of one time you ignored instinct. What was the cost?
- ❖ Can you distinguish between instinct and fear in your own life?
- ❖ How can you practice trusting your gut without dismissing logic?

Chapter - Six
Instinct in Relationships

They say love is blind. But let's be honest: most of the time, it's not blind — it's just wearing tinted sunglasses and refusing to take them off even when the room gets dark. And this is where instinct enters, like that irritating-but-honest friend who keeps saying: "Hey, something feels off here."

When it comes to relationships — friendships, romances, even family ties — instinct plays a much bigger role than we admit. It's the quiet background music that tells you whether the story you're living is a rom-com, a thriller, or a horror movie.

The Whisper We Ignore

Here's the irony: in relationships, instinct usually speaks first. Before you analyse compatibility, before you check horoscopes or love languages, before you stalk their Instagram — your gut has already whispered something. The problem? Most of us hit "mute."

- You meet someone, they say all the right things, but something feels fake. You ignore it. Months later, you discover the mask.

- You meet another person, nothing flashy, but something feels warm, safe, familiar. You ignore it because "no sparks." Years later, you realise that was stability disguised as boring.

Instinct doesn't shout; it nudges. The question is: do you listen?

Red Flags Your Instinct Notices First

Logic might take months to identify red flags, but instinct spots them instantly.

- The overly charming partner who flatters everyone — your gut whispers: This isn't special, it's a script.
- The friend who laughs at your pain but never at their own — your gut whispers: This isn't friendship, it's mockery.
- The "perfect" lover who somehow always makes you feel guilty — your gut whispers: Manipulation alert.

The sad part? We often explain these away with logic: "Oh, maybe I'm overreacting," "Everyone has flaws," "But they're so nice otherwise." Instinct doesn't do PR. It just tells you the raw truth.

The Detective in Disguise

Your instinct is basically a detective working overtime. It notices body language, tone, micro-expressions — things your conscious mind skips. The way someone avoids eye contact, how they answer questions too quickly, and how they suddenly change their laugh around different people. These clues feed into a subconscious verdict: trust or don't trust.

Ever wonder why your best friend instantly hates your new partner without a "logical" reason? That's instinct at work. Sometimes others' instincts see what our emotions refuse to.

The Illusion of Romantic Checklists

In relationships, society loves checklists. Tall, fair, rich, stable. Cute couple photos. "Power couple" vibes. But instinct doesn't care about checklists. It cares about energy.

I once knew a girl who married someone who ticked all the boxes — educated, rich, polite. On paper, he was "perfect." But her instinct never trusted him. Within three years, the cracks showed: control, gaslighting, manipulation. Her logic had been dazzled by the résumé; her instinct had seen the truth from day one.

Lesson? Don't outsource relationships to Excel sheets.

Love vs. Lust vs. Loyalty

- Lust screams, This is amazing, let's do this now.
- Love whispers, This feels right. I want to build here.
- Loyalty proves, I'm staying, even when it's messy.

Instinct helps separate these three. Lust is loud, love is steady, loyalty is tested. Without instinct, it's easy to confuse temporary sparks with lifelong fire.

Friendships and Instinct

Romance gets the spotlight, but instinct works in friendships too.

Ever had a "friend" who was fun at parties but exhausting in private? Instinct spotted the imbalance long before your mind admitted it. Or maybe you met someone briefly, but felt they were safe enough to trust with secrets. That's instinct as a shortcut — saving you years of testing.

When Instinct Saves Your Heart

Instinct doesn't just apply to relationships — it applies to the choices we make every day. While writing this book, there were moments I almost deleted whole sections. Logic told me they were messy, unpolished, imperfect. My gut told me to keep going. The words you're reading exist because instinct was right.

But I've also ignored instinct. A project that looked flawless on paper. An opportunity that glittered like a shortcut. Each time, my gut raised the alarm, and each time I buried it under logic. Months later, both collapsed exactly the way instinct had warned. Logic had the data, but instinct had the truth.

Why We Ignore Instinct

So why do we ignore it? Three reasons:

1. Societal Pressure — "He's perfect on paper, don't be stupid."
2. Fear of Being Alone — We'd rather silence instinct than face loneliness.
3. Hope for Change — We think red flags are just "temporary." Spoiler: they're not.

Ignoring instinct usually costs more than listening to it.

Instinct vs. Logic in Relationships

Logic asks: Do they earn well? Are they reliable? Do our lifestyles match?

Instinct asks: Do I feel safe? Do I feel respected? Do I feel at peace?

Both matter. Logic builds stability; instinct builds trust. One without the other is a disaster. A purely logical relationship feels like a business contract. A purely instinctive one feels like a roller coaster with no seatbelt. Balance is survival.

Instinct in Breakups

Interestingly, instinct also shows up at the end. Most people sense the death of a relationship long before the breakup. Conversations feel forced, affection feels absent, energy feels heavy. Instinct says: It's over. But we drag it out, using logic to justify: "Maybe it's just a phase." Months later, the inevitable happens — and instinct smirks, Told you so.

Building Trust with Instinct

The more you listen, the sharper it gets. Start small:

- Notice your gut reaction when meeting new people.
- Write down your first impressions.
- check them months later against reality.

You'll be surprised how often instinct got it right.

Pause and Reflect

- Think of a friend or partner your instinct warned you about. What happened when you ignored it?
- Recall someone you trusted instantly. Did your instinct prove correct?
- In your relationships, do you lean on logic first or instinct first? How has that shaped your experiences?
- What's one relationship mistake you could have avoided if you had trusted your gut?

Chapter - Seven
Instinct and Society

Humans love to think of themselves as rational beings, driven by intelligence, reason, and civilisation. But scratch the surface, and you'll find we're not as far from animals as we'd like to believe. In fact, much of society still runs on instinct — just dressed up in fancier clothes.

One person starts running in a crowd, and suddenly dozens follow, no questions asked. A new "life hack" goes viral on social media, and suddenly, millions are pouring Coke into toilets because some stranger said it works. That's herd instinct, alive and kicking. Society is basically a zoo where the animals think they're philosophers.

Herd Instinct: The Copy-Paste Syndrome

Instinct thrives in groups. You'd think a crowd makes us smarter, but more often than not, it makes us dumber. This is herd instinct — monkey see, monkey do, except the monkey has a smartphone.

Examples Are Everywhere:

- **Sales & Discounts:** One person rushes into a store because of a "50% OFF" sign. Within minutes, the shop is packed. Half of them don't even know what they're buying.

- **Social media Trends:** Someone pours ice water on their head, suddenly millions are doing it. For a cause? Sometimes. For attention? Mostly. By the way, I also follow this
- **Panic Situations:** A fire alarm goes off. Even if it's a drill, nobody waits for logic. Instinct takes over: RUN.

The same instinct saves lives during real danger but also creates chaos in false alarms. Society often operates on copy-paste reactions more often than it admits.

The Varieties of Instinct in Society

Humans aren't driven by just one instinct — we come pre-installed with several "apps" we never asked for. Here are a few:

1. **Survival Instinct**

   Fight-or-flight. Perfect when you're facing a real tiger. Less useful when the "tiger" is your Wi-Fi lagging for 5 seconds.

2. **Parental/Caregiving Instinct**

   That supernatural radar parents have. Moms especially. A child lies, and somehow, she knows before the lie even finishes leaving their mouth. Science calls it intuition; kids call it witchcraft.

3. **Social/Herd Instinct**

   The glue of communities. It keeps us connected, but it also explains why mobs form faster than you can say "WhatsApp forward."

4. **Sexual/Reproductive Instinct**

   Nature's billboard screaming: "Continue the species." Subtle? Not at all. Half of Tinder runs purely on this.

5. **Territorial Instinct**

   That invisible "my spot" feeling. Whether it's a seat in class, a cubicle at work, or your corner of the bed, humans are basically cats with better hairstyles.

6. **Curiosity Instinct**

   The reason kids shove fingers into sockets and adults still click on obvious clickbait. Without it, no discoveries. With too much of it, hospital bills.

Tradition: Herd Instinct in Formal Clothes

Half of what we call "culture" is basically herd instinct passed down with a bow tie. People say, "This is tradition." Translation: We've been copy-pasting this for generations without asking why.

Festivals, rituals, and customs can be beautiful — they bring community, identity, and a sense of meaning. But the danger comes when we stop questioning whether the practice still serves a purpose. Lighting lamps? Meaningful. Denying education to women because of "tradition"? Pure herd instinct dressed up as morality.

Mob Mentality: Logic on Vacation

Have you ever noticed how individuals who are calm and reasonable alone suddenly become aggressive, loud, and irrational in a crowd? That's mob mentality. Once instinct takes the wheel, logic is duct-taped in the trunk.

Mobs don't debate. They don't check evidence. They act. And the scariest part? The same instinct that unites a society in celebrations can unite it in destruction. History is full of both: parades of joy and riots of hate, both fuelled by the same herd wiring.

The Double-Edged Sword

Instinct in society isn't all bad. Without it, humans wouldn't have survived disasters. Imagine a stampede caused by a fire — herd instinct saves lives because nobody stops to argue about whether the flames are real.

But the same instinct causes chaos when there is no fire, only fear. Entire economies have crashed because of mass panic. Stock markets fall not always because companies fail, but because instinct tells millions of investors to pull out at the same time.

A Personal Observation

I once watched a small protest in my city. It began with ten people, chanting peacefully. Within an hour, hundreds joined, many with no idea what the protest was even about. Some were shouting slogans that didn't even match the cause. That's society on instinct: follow first, understand later.

Why We Fall for It

- **Fear:** When scared, instinct takes charge before logic even wakes up.
- **Belonging:** We crave connection, and following the crowd feels safer than standing alone.
- **Convenience:** Thinking is hard. Copying is easy.

Balancing Instinct with Logic

Society needs instinct — it keeps us alive and connected. But it also needs logic, or else we spiral into chaos. The trick isn't killing instinct, but balancing it.

- **Instinct says:** Run with the crowd.
- **Logic says:** Wait, why are we running?
- **Balance says:** check if there's smoke first, then run if necessary.

Pause and Reflect

- ❖ When was the last time you followed the crowd without thinking? Did it help, or just waste your time?
- ❖ Which instinct do you notice most in yourself — survival, social, curiosity, or another?
- ❖ Think about one tradition you follow. Does it actually make sense, or is it just autopilot?
- ❖ How can you let instinct guide you without letting it hijack your choices?

Chapter - Eight

The Limits of Instinct

Instinct gets a lot of praise. We glorify it in quotes: "Trust your gut." "Follow your intuition." "Your first feeling is always right." Sounds inspiring, right? But let's be real: instinct is not some magical superhero that saves you from every bad decision. Sometimes it's just fear in disguise. Sometimes it's bias pretending to be wisdom. And sometimes, it's just your stomach growling and tricking you into thinking you're having a "gut feeling."

Instinct is powerful, but it has limits. If you worship it blindly, it can wreck your relationships, your career, even your peace of mind.

Why Instinct Feels So Convincing

The problem with instinct isn't that it's always wrong. The problem is that it feels so right. Your gut tells you something, and because it arrives fast and strong, you assume it must be true. But feelings aren't facts. Just because something feels real doesn't mean it is.

Think about fear. Fear feels real even when the danger isn't. Afraid of speaking on stage? Your heart races, palms sweat — but nobody in the audience has a gun pointed at you. That's instinct confusing embarrassment with death.

Instinct Gets Hijacked by Fear

Fear loves hijacking instinct. Back in the jungle days, it was useful. A rustle in the bushes? Assume it's a predator and run. Better safe than sorry. But in modern life, the "bushes" are emails, exams, or dating apps. Fear convinces instinct that everything is dangerous. Suddenly, you're running from shadows.

- **Example:** You feel a gut warning that your partner is cheating. Reality? They just forgot to reply to a text. Fear wore instinct's costume and fooled you.

Instinct Confuses Bias with Truth

Here's the ugly side: instinct isn't pure. It's shaped by culture, upbringing, and stereotypes.

- Instinct might tell you not to trust someone because of how they look, dress, or speak. But that's not wisdom — that's bias you absorbed from your environment.
- Instinct might make you uncomfortable around someone from a background you don't understand. Again, not true. Just prejudice disguised as intuition.

Without logic to filter it, instinct can become a polite name for discrimination.

Instinct Ignores Evidence

Ever had a strong feeling about something, ignored all the facts, and later regretted it? That's the instinct's ego.

- You "felt" the stock market was going up, ignored the data, and lost money.
- You "knew" this person was "the one," ignored all red flags, and ended up in therapy.

Instinct doesn't always care about reality; it cares about speed. And speed isn't always accuracy.

Instinct Thrives on Overconfidence

Another trap: instinct often makes you overconfident. Because it feels right, you assume it must be right. That's why people say, "I don't need data, I just know." Spoiler: they usually don't.

History is full of disasters caused by overconfidence in instinct — from failed business empires to wars started on "gut feelings." Confidence feels good; correctness actually matters.

Manipulated Instincts

Worst of all, instinct is easy to manipulate. Advertisers do it every day. They use colours, music, scarcity tricks, and emotional triggers to hijack your instincts. Politicians use fear, pride, and belonging to make entire societies follow them without thinking.

If instinct were foolproof, propaganda wouldn't work. But it does. Which means instinct can be hacked.

Personal Story: When My Instinct Lied

I've lived with anxiety issues since childhood. Back then, it showed up as constant worry about things that never actually happened. As I grew older, it evolved into something heavier: Generalised Anxiety Disorder. One place it hits me hardest is driving. The moment I sit behind the wheel, my gut screams that something terrible will happen — that I'll lose control, that an accident is waiting. It feels like instinct, but it isn't. It's anxiety wearing instinct's clothes. The truth is, most of the time, nothing happens at all. The road is just the road.

And yet, even as I write this book, I haven't overcome that fear. I know I should have gone to a psychologist or psychiatrist, but I still haven't. That doesn't make the point weaker — it makes it sharper: instinct isn't flawless, and neither are we. It needs fact-checking, support, and sometimes the courage to seek help we keep postponing. And maybe writing this book is my first step toward that courage.

Balancing Instinct with Logic

So, should we ignore instinct? No. That would be stupid. Instinct has saved countless lives and continues to guide us daily. The trick isn't throwing it away — it's balancing it with logic.

- **Instinct says:** Don't trust this person.
- **Logic asks:** Why? What evidence supports this?
- **Together:** a decision rooted in both safety and clarity.

Instinct Isn't Magic, It's Data

Think of instinct as your brain's fast-forward button. It's built from experience, memory, and subconscious pattern recognition. It feels magical, but really, it's data compressed into a shortcut. The catch? If your data is flawed (bias, trauma, fear), your instinct will be flawed too.

Why People Romanticise Instinct

People love instinct because it feels rebellious. Logic is boring, slow, and full of Excel sheets. Instinct is dramatic—"I trusted my gut and flew to another country, and everything worked out!" Great story. But notice how the failures don't go viral: "I trusted my gut, invested in a shady startup, and now I'm broke." Not as inspirational.

Pause and Reflect

- ❖ Recall a time your instinct turned out wrong. What did it cost you?
- ❖ Think of one judgment you made instantly about someone. Was it fair, or just biased?
- ❖ Have you ever been manipulated because someone played on your instincts (fear, attraction, belonging)?
- ❖ How can you double-check instinct with logic before acting?

Part III – Intent

Chapter - Nine
Defining Intent

Logic clears the fog. Instinct whispers directions. But intent? Intent decides why you're even on the road in the first place. It's the fuel, the hidden driver, the answer to the most irritating and yet most important question in life: Why?

People talk about logic and instinct all the time. They show up in books, psychology experiments, and even corporate training sessions. But intent doesn't get the same spotlight. Maybe because it's uncomfortable. Logic and instinct can be observed; intent has to be admitted. And most people don't like admitting why they really do what they do.

What Is Intent, really?

At its simplest, intent is the purpose behind an action. Not the action itself — the reason.

- Two people can do the same thing with entirely different intents.
- One donates money for claps on Instagram. Another donates quietly to actually help.

- One friend "supports" you to keep you dependent. Another supports you because they want to see you grow.

On the outside, both look identical. On the inside, intent changes everything.

Intent as the Hidden Script

Think of life as a movie. Logic is the script supervisor. Instinct is the actor improvising lines. But intent? The intent is the director shouting, "This is the story we're telling."

Even when we're not conscious of it, intent is always present. Why are you working this job? Why are you in this relationship? Why are you posting that selfie? There's always a "why," whether we acknowledge it or not.

The Difference Between Action and Intent

Actions are visible. Intent is invisible — until outcomes reveal it.

Example:

- A politician passes a law "for the people." Intent? Maybe justice, maybe votes.
- A friend gives advice. Intent? Maybe care, maybe control.
- You write a book. Intent? Maybe legacy, maybe money, maybe both.

The same action, judged differently, once intent is revealed.

Story: The ₹50,000 Lesson

Once, I booked a plot of land and paid a token amount of ₹50,000. Later, I cancelled. The agent returned only ₹45,000, keeping ₹5,000 casually — and this guy drove a Land Rover. His words were sympathetic, his smile polite, but his intent was profit, not honesty.

That's how intent shows its true face. Not in words, but in outcomes.

Money, Intent, and Truth

Let's be honest: money and intent are married. Money reveals intent faster than anything else.

- Someone may gift you expensive things not because they care, but because they want control.
- A business may claim "customer first," but its intent might be profit at any cost.
- Even with ourselves — are we saving money for security, or for showing off? Intent defines the meaning.

Money isn't evil. It's neutral. Intent decides whether it becomes a tool for growth or a weapon for greed.

My Intent With This Book

Let me admit something: yes, I'd love it if this book sells. Money is nice. But that's not my main intent. I intend to leave something behind. To turn my overthinking, my sarcasm, my reflections into something that might help at least one reader.

That's the difference. Intent doesn't need to be holy. It just needs to be clear.

Intent in Relationships

Intent makes or breaks relationships.

- A partner may "care" by checking your phone—intent is control, not love.
- A friend may push you hard — the intent is to help you grow, not to belittle.
- Families may "sacrifice" for you — intent may be love, or guilt, or obligation.

We often get confused because we judge actions alone. But actions are costumes. Intent is the actor beneath.

Intent as the Mirror

Intent reveals character. You can fake words, you can fake actions for a while, but intent always leaks through. Like water through cracks. Sooner or later, people see it.

That's why clear intent is freeing. You don't need to over-explain yourself. People may still misunderstand, but if your intent is pure, you sleep peacefully at night.

The Three Friends: Mirror, Ladder, Shield

I once came across an Instagram reel that said you need three types of friends:

1. **The Mirror** — the one who reflects your truth, even when it's ugly.
2. **The Ladder** — the one who's ahead of you, pulling you upward.
3. **The Shield** — the one who stands by you in storms.

That's intent in action. Each role is defined not by what they do, but by why they do it.

When Intent Gets Twisted

Of course, not everyone has good intent. Some people smile while plotting. Some people "help" while secretly competing. Some people say "I love you" while their intent is ownership.

That's why aligning your logic and instinct with intent is crucial. Your brain sees patterns. Your gut feels energy. Together, they uncover what intent words try to hide.

The Finger Rule

Sometimes, you'll have the purest intent and still get misunderstood. People will twist it, doubt it, misuse it. What do you do? You don't explain endlessly. You don't beg to be understood. You either protect your peace — or, when necessary, show them the universal language of the middle finger and move on.

Pause and Reflect

- Recall a time when someone's intent toward you wasn't what it seemed. How did you find out?
- Think about your own intent in a recent situation—was it pure, or mixed with hidden motives?
- Who are your "mirror, ladder, and shield" friends right now? Do you have all three?
- Has jealousy ever poisoned your intent toward someone? How could you flip that into growth?

Chapter - Ten
Aligning Intent with Logic and Instinct

If logic is the map, and instinct is the traveller's gut feeling about which turn to take, then intent is the destination itself. Without a clear destination, the map is pointless, and the traveller just wanders aimlessly. That's why alignment matters. Logic, instinct, and intent can each work alone — but if they don't line up, your life becomes a circus where every clown pulls in a different direction.

Why Alignment Matters

Picture This:

- **Logic says:** "This job is stable."
- **Instinct says:** "This job feels soul-crushing."
- **Intent says:** "I want freedom, not just a paycheque."

If you follow only logic, you end up with stability and misery. If you follow only instinct, you might quit recklessly. If you follow only intent, you may chase freedom with no plan. But when they align? You find a role that's stable, fulfilling, and matches your long-term purpose. That's not luck — that's alignment.

The Danger of Misalignment

1. **Logic Without Instinct or Intent**

   Imagine building a perfect five-year plan with spreadsheets, KPIs, and smart goals — but your intent is unclear. You'll work hard, maybe succeed, but feel empty. Success without intent tastes like cardboard.

2. **Instinct Without Logic or Intent**

   You "just feel" like quitting your job and moving abroad. But you didn't check visas, finances, or cultural realities. You'll get adventure, yes, but also chaos. Instinct alone is like jumping without checking if there's water in the pool.

3. **Intent Without Logic or Instinct**

   You know your purpose — say, becoming a writer. But you ignore logic (skills, editing, publishing) and instinct (audience vibes). The result? Passionate rants that never become books. Intent alone is just daydreaming with confidence.

When Alignment Works

Think about the best decisions of your life. Chances are, all three lined up.

- You moved to a new city not just because logic said it had opportunities, not just because instinct said it felt exciting, but also because you intended to grow.

- You chose a relationship not just because instinct screamed "sparks!" but because logic confirmed compatibility and intent ensured you wanted the same future.

That's alignment: head, heart, and purpose shaking hands.

The Triangle of Decision-Making

Visualise it as a triangle:

- One corner is Logic (clarity, evidence).
- One corner is Instinct (feelings, intuition).
- One corner is Intent (purpose, why).

If one side is missing, the triangle collapses. Balance keeps it strong.

Case Study: Money Choices

Take money as an example.

- **Logic says:** "Save, invest, don't buy things you don't need."
- **Instinct says:** "Something about this scheme feels shady, even though the numbers look good."
- **Intent says:** "Am I building wealth for security, or just for flexing on Instagram?"

You can see how the same money means totally different things depending on intent. Alignment keeps money as a tool, not a trap.

Case Study: Relationships

Relationships without alignment are disasters in disguise.

- **Logic may say:** "This person is reliable."
- **Instinct may whisper:** "Something feels off."
- **Intent may scream:** "I just want love, I don't care about the rest."

When these three don't agree, heartbreak is inevitable. You either compromise logic for lust, ignore instinct for fantasy, or bend intent just to avoid loneliness. Alignment prevents these traps by making sure the "why" matches both the "what" and the "how."

My Own Misalignment

I'll admit it: I've made choices where logic was screaming at me, instinct was quietly warning me, and intent… well, intent was on vacation. The result? Disaster. Whether it was trusting the wrong people or investing in the wrong places, misalignment always cost me peace.

But when I started asking all three voices — logic, instinct, and intent — to sit at the same table before deciding, life got lighter. Not easier, but lighter. Because even tough decisions felt rooted. And still, I know I will make mistakes — because I'm human. Writing this book doesn't grant me immunity from that. It just makes me a little more aware when I do.

Alignment Isn't Perfection

Important: alignment doesn't mean every decision becomes a fairy tale. Life is messy. But aligned decisions reduce regret. Even if things go wrong, you know why you chose that path. That clarity alone is worth it.

Practical Ways to Align the Three

1. **Ask the Triple Question**
    - Does it make sense logically?
    - Does it feel right instinctively?
    - Does it match my intent?
    - If two out of three scream "no," don't do it.
2. **Set Time Boundaries**

    Logic loves endless analysis. Instinct loves rushing. Intent loves dreaming. Balance them by setting decision deadlines.
3. **Check Your Why Twice**

    Sometimes logic and instinct agree, but your intent is off. Example: You buy a car. Logic: good deal. Instinct: feels right. Intent: just showing off. Misaligned intent makes even good decisions hollow.
4. **Review Outcomes**

    After decisions, check: did my alignment work? If not, which corner was missing? This reflection sharpens future alignment.

Story: The Writing Crossroads

When I was deep into writing this book, I hit a wall. Logic said: the draft is messy; it needs more structure. Instinct said: the core idea is alive, don't kill it yet. Intent said: My purpose isn't perfection, it's connection. Alignment said: Keep going, even if imperfect. I did — and while the process wasn't smooth, it gave me pages that mattered. Without alignment, I would have either abandoned the book out of fear or forced it into something lifeless.

Pause and Reflect

- Think of your last big decision. Did you check it against all three — logic, instinct, and intent?
- Where do you usually lean more — logic, instinct, or intent? Has it helped or hurt you?
- Recall one mistake caused by misalignment. Which part was missing?
- What area of your life right now (career, money, relationships) needs better alignment?

Chapter - Eleven
Living with Clear Intent

We've talked about logic, we've explored instinct, and we've ripped open intent. But now comes the real test: living it. Because knowing something is useless if it just sits in your head like an unopened app. Clear intent isn't just a concept — it's a way of moving through life. And it's a tough one.

Most people don't live with intent. They live on autopilot. They follow routines, traditions, jobs, and even relationships without asking why. Days blur into weeks, weeks into years, and suddenly they wake up wondering, How the hell did I get here?

Living with clear intent is the antidote. It doesn't make life easier, but it makes life yours.

What Does Clear Intent Mean?

Clear intent is not about perfection. It's not about turning into a saint who never makes mistakes. It's about being honest with yourself.

- **Clear Intent Says:** "I'm choosing this job because I value security right now."
- **Hidden Intent Says:** "I'm choosing this job because society told me it's respectable, but I'll pretend it's passion."

- **Clear Intent Says:** "I want this relationship because I genuinely love this person."
- **Hidden Intent Says:** "I want this relationship because I'm scared of being alone, but I'll call it love."

The actions may look the same, but the energy behind them feels completely different.

Freedom in Honesty

The biggest gift of clear intent is freedom. Not freedom from problems — those will always exist — but freedom from pretending. When you're honest about your intent, you don't have to juggle masks. You don't waste energy maintaining an image.

For example:

- If your intent is money, admit it. There's no shame. Just own it.
- If your intent is love, admit it. Don't disguise it as "networking" or "friendship."
- If your intent is growth, admit it. Even if others don't understand.

People may still judge you, but at least you're not judging yourself.

Why Hidden Intent Is Dangerous

Hidden intent eats away at peace. It creates a gap between what you say and what you actually want. That gap becomes stress, resentment, even regret.

Think of workplaces. A boss says, "We care about employees." Intent? Profits. Employees feel the mismatch. Or relationships: someone says, "I'm here for you," but their intent is control. The mismatch eventually blows up.

Living with clear intent avoids this trap.

My Own Realisation

I'll admit — I wasn't always clear. I used to clap for friends while secretly feeling jealous. My intent wasn't pure. Over time, I realised envy wasn't hurting them, it was eating me. I had two choices: hide it or flip it. I chose to flip it. Now, when a friend succeeds, I intend to learn, not compete. Life feels lighter that way.

When People Misunderstand Your Intent

Here's the catch: even when your intent is pure, people will sometimes twist it. They'll doubt you, misuse you, or project their insecurities on you. That's normal. Your job isn't to convince everyone. Your job is to keep your intent clear for yourself.

And when people refuse to see it? Walk away. Or, if necessary, use the universal language of the middle finger and move on.

Intent and Everyday Choices

Clear intent isn't just for big life decisions. It applies to daily choices:

- Why am I saying yes to this plan? Because I want to, or because I'm scared to disappoint?

- Why am I posting this picture? Because I like it, or because I crave validation?
- Why am I working late? Because I'm ambitious, or because I don't know how to set boundaries?

These small checks keep life aligned.

Intent vs. Outcome

Important truth: clear intent doesn't guarantee success. You can do everything with the right heart and still fail. But unclear intent almost always guarantees regret. Success is unpredictable. Intent is within your control.

How to Build Clear Intent

1. **Ask "Why" Relentlessly**

   Before every major choice, ask yourself why. If the answer is vague, dig deeper.

2. **Write It Down**

   Sometimes intent hides until you write it. Journaling forces honesty.

3. **Catch the Excuses**

   If you're saying, "I had no choice," stop. That's usually a cover for unclear intent.

4. **Accept Imperfection**

   Clear intent doesn't mean noble intent. It means honest intent. Even selfishness, when admitted, is less toxic than fake generosity.

Story: Two Entrepreneurs

I once met two entrepreneurs. Both started businesses. Both worked hard. One's intent was to make quick money. The other's intent was to solve a real problem. Guess who lasted longer? The second one. The first made money fast, but burned out. Why? Because intent decides whether your fuel is durable or temporary.

Legacy of Intent

At the end of life, people may forget your possessions, your titles, even your achievements. But they'll remember your intent. Did you live with bitterness or generosity? With envy or encouragement? With selfishness or contribution? That's the story that sticks.

Pause and Reflect

- What's one area of your life right now where your intent is unclear?
- Recall a time when your intent was misunderstood. Did you fight to explain, or did you protect your peace?
- How do you want people to remember your intent—not your achievements, but your energy?
- What's one small choice today you can make with clearer intent?

Part IV – Balance & Action

Chapter - Twelve
Finding Your Balance

Life isn't about choosing Logic over Instinct, or Instinct over Intent. It's about not letting one of them hijack the steering wheel while the others are duct-taped in the backseat. Balance isn't glamorous, but it's survival.

Too much logic, and you turn into a robot, paralysed by spreadsheets. Too much instinct, and you're a gambler chasing vibes until disaster strikes. Too much intent, and you risk becoming a philosopher who dreams but never moves. Balance doesn't mean perfection; it means refusing to let one voice drown out the others.

What Balance Really Looks Like

Balance isn't some mystical state where your chakras align and birds start singing. It's practical. It looks like this:

- **Logic:** "This job pays well, has growth."
- **Instinct:** "The manager feels shady, don't trust."
- **Intent:** "I want stability for a few years."

Balanced Decision: Take the job, but keep your eyes open, save money, and build an exit strategy.

Or In Relationships:

- **Logic:** "We share values, we're compatible."
- **Instinct:** "Something feels genuine here."
- **Intent:** "I want to build, not just date for fun."
- **Balanced choice:** commit with awareness, not blind passion or forced duty.

Balance Is Messy But Doable

My Phases of Imbalance

I've lived all three extremes:

- **Too Logical:** I overanalysed everything — career, friendships, even which toothpaste to buy. Result? Paralysis. Opportunities slipped while I was still calculating.
- **Too Instinctive:** I dove into decisions because "it felt right." Spoiler: many didn't feel right later when the overthinking kicked in.
- **Too Intent-Focused:** I dreamed of impact, legacy, purpose — but ignored the small logical steps needed. I ended up stuck in vision with no execution.

Only when I started asking: What does my head say? What does my gut say? What does my heart want? — Did things start balancing out?

Balance ≠ Perfection

Important truth: balance doesn't mean you'll never stumble. It means when you do, you can recalibrate faster. Think of it like driving. You don't hold the steering wheel perfectly straight all the time. You make small corrections. Balance in life works the same way.

The Car Analogy

Life is like driving a car:

- Logic is the GPS — it shows the map.
- Instinct is your reflex — when a dog jumps in front, you swerve.
- Intent is your destination — the reason you're on the road.

No GPS? You're lost. No reflex? You crash. No destination? You're just wasting petrol.

Why Balance Feels Boring

People hate balance because it doesn't make for great stories. Nobody brags, "I lived moderately and avoided disasters." Instead, stories glorify extremes: the genius who only trusted logic, the wild risk-taker who only followed instinct, the visionary who only chased intent. But for every one success story, thousands of failures never make the headlines. Balance isn't sexy, but it's sustainable.

How to Practice Balance

1. **Daily check-ins. Ask:**

   Am I leaning too much on one voice today? For example, am I only calculating and ignoring feelings? Or only following vibes without a plan?

2. **Pause Before Big Choices**

   Don't decide until you've run the "logic–instinct–intent" test.

3. **Learn From Imbalance**

   Every failure teaches which voice you ignored. Reflect, adjust, move forward.

4. **Surround Yourself with Balance**

   Friends who are too much like you reinforce imbalance. Balance-seeking people challenge you.

Story: The Impulse Text

I once sent a long, emotional text because "my gut told me to be honest." Logic said wait, intent wasn't clear. The message landed wrong, and the silence after said it all. Balance would've said: *"Sleep on it, send it tomorrow."*

Story: The Unsent Message

On the flip side, I've stayed silent when I should have spoken. Logic said, *"Don't create drama."* Instinct whispered, *"Say it now."* Intent wanted honesty. I ignored both. The message was never sent, the moment passed, and regret moved in. Balance would've said: *"Speak with care, not silence."*

Balance and Growth

Balance isn't static. What's balanced today might not be tomorrow. Early in life, you may lean on logic (build skills, earn stability). Later, instinct may guide you into risks. Then the intent becomes louder (legacy, meaning). Balance shifts with seasons. The trick is to notice the shift and adjust.

The Cost of Ignoring Balance

- **All Logic:** You live "safe," but regret missed chances.
- **All Instinct:** You chase highs, but burn out.
- **All Intent:** You dream, but starve.

Balance isn't optional. It's survival with dignity.

Pause and Reflect

- ❖ Are you running more on logic, instinct, or intent these days? What's the cost?
- ❖ Think of your last failure. Which part was missing — logic, instinct, or intent?
- ❖ What does balance look like in your daily decisions?
- ❖ Where can you practice small corrections instead of waiting for big crashes?

Chapter - Thirteen

Decision-Making in Action

Here's an uncomfortable truth: most people don't actually make decisions. They delay, avoid, outsource, or let circumstances choose for them. Then, when things go wrong, they blame "fate" or "destiny." Sorry, but fate didn't waste three years of your life — your indecision did.

Logic, instinct, and intent are powerful tools, but they mean nothing if you don't act. A map, a compass, and a destination are useless if you refuse to start walking. Decision-making is where theory meets reality.

Why We Avoid Decisions

1. **Fear of Being Wrong**

   We think: If I decide and fail, I'll look stupid. So we stay stuck, convincing ourselves that "waiting for the right moment" is wise. Reality? We're just scared.

2. **Too Many Choices**

   Modern life gives us endless options — careers, relationships, even toothpaste brands. Choice overload paralyses us. Ironically, more freedom often means less action.

3. **Overthinking**

   Logic sometimes goes rogue. You create spreadsheets, pros-and-cons lists, and even consult tarot cards — until opportunities vanish while you're still calculating.

4. **Borrowed Intent**

   Sometimes we don't decide because we're not clear on what we want. We're living on borrowed time—chasing careers parents chose, partners society approves, lifestyles Instagram sells.

The Cost of Indecision

Indecision is not neutral. It's a decision to let others decide for you. The job you didn't take, someone else did. The partner you hesitated on, someone else married. The opportunity you postponed, expired.

Life punishes hesitation more than mistakes. Mistakes teach. Hesitation leaves you with nothing.

- **Logic, Instinct, Intent in Action**

  Let's break it down with real examples.

- **Health Decision**
- **Logic:** "The diet chart says cut all carbs immediately."
- **Instinct:** "This feels extreme; I'll burn out."
- **Intent:** "I want sustainable health, not short-term punishment."

- **Action:** Maybe you don't follow the crash diet at all. Instead, you start by cutting sugar or reducing portions, something you can actually sustain. Small steps that respect logic, instinct, and intent together.
- **Relationships**
  - **Logic:** "They're reliable, stable."
  - **Instinct:** "Something feels off."
  - **Intent:** "I want genuine love, not just companionship."
  - **Action:** Instead of dragging it for years, you either commit with clarity or walk away.
- **Money**
  - **Logic:** "This investment looks profitable."
  - **Instinct:** "Feels shady."
  - **Intent:** "I want long-term security."
  - **Action:** You skip the "too good to be true" scheme and choose safer, boring stability.

The Myth of the Perfect Decision

We wait for the "perfect" choice. Spoiler: it doesn't exist. Every decision has risk. Even "safe" ones. The trick is not to avoid risk, but to choose risks aligned with your values.

- Wrong decision with clear intent = lesson.
- Right decision with unclear intent = regret.
- No decision at all = stagnation.

Small Decisions, Big Impact

We think only big decisions matter, but small ones shape life too.

- Saying yes to coffee with a stranger may open a network.
- Choosing to read instead of scrolling may shape your mindset.
- Deciding to speak up in a meeting may change your career trajectory.

Every small decision trains your decision-making muscle. Weak muscles collapse under a big weight.

Instinct in Action

Sometimes, instinct is faster than logic and more accurate. Think about driving. You don't calculate angles before swerving to avoid an accident. Instinct saves you. Same with people — sometimes your gut calls it before evidence arrives.

But instinct alone is risky. That's why reflection after action matters. You refine instinct by checking: Was my gut right this time?

Intent in Action

Intent keeps you honest. Why are you really making this decision? Is it fear, pressure, or clarity?

- Taking a high-paying job out of fear of judgment? That intent will poison the joy.
- Marrying someone because you're scared of loneliness? That intent will haunt you later.
- Starting a business with the intent to grow, not just show off? That intent will carry you through failure.

Action without intent is just movement. Intent makes it meaningful.

My Own Lesson in Action

While writing this book, I kept circling one chapter for weeks. Logic told me it needed polish. Instinct whispered it was fine. Intent said: move forward. I stalled anyway, rewriting the same lines over and over. In the end, nothing collapsed but my momentum. Lesson learned: delay doesn't create clarity — it just feeds doubt.

How to Make Decisions Faster

1. **The 2/3 Rule**

   If two out of three (logic, instinct, intent) agree, go for it. Don't wait for perfection.

2. **Set Deadlines**

   Big choices need time, but not infinite time. Decide within a set window, or you'll lose momentum.

3. **Default to Action**

   When in doubt, choose movement over stagnation. You can adjust later, but you can't adjust a decision you never made.

4. **Check Regret Potential**

   Ask: If I don't do this, will I regret it in 5 years? If yes, act.

Decision-Making Is a Habit

Like muscles, decision-making gets stronger with use. Start with small things: what to eat, what to read, how to spend an hour. Build confidence in choosing. Then, when life throws big ones, you won't freeze.

Pause and Reflect

- What's one decision you've been avoiding? Which voice — logic, instinct, or intent — are you ignoring?
- Think of your last "wrong" decision. Was it truly wrong, or just misaligned?
- Where in life do you let others', intent overrule your own?
- What's one small decision you can make today to build your decision muscle?

Chapter - Fourteen
Living Intentionally

Knowing about intent is one thing. Living intentionally? That's a whole different battlefield. It's like the difference between reading a cookbook and actually cooking dinner without burning the kitchen down. Everyone says they want to live intentionally — focus on purpose, cut out the noise, design their own life. But when the alarm rings at 6 a.m., Instagram wins over meditation, and "Netflix autoplay" defeats "personal growth." I know, because I've done it — told myself *"Just five minutes online"* and then wondered how the sun set while my growth plan was still on pause. Living intentionally isn't about being perfect. It's about being deliberate. It's about asking *why* before saying yes, and asking *what for* before saying no. I'm not perfect at this either. Even while writing this book with the help of GPT, I've had to face my own patterns of rushing or resisting. Which only means I'll need to come back to these questions, time to time, to reflect and realign myself.

What Living Intentionally Is (and Isn't)

- It isn't about having every hour of your life scheduled like a military boot camp.
- It isn't about turning into some productivity robot who never wastes time.
- It isn't about posting #intentional captions while secretly being miserable.

Living Intentionally Is About Alignment

- Aligning your actions with your intent.
- Aligning your choices with your values.
- Aligning your time with what actually matters to you.

Why We Don't Live Intentionally

1. **Autopilot Living**

   Society trains us to follow scripts: school → job → marriage → kids → retirement. Nothing wrong with that path if it's yours. But most people never stop to ask if it actually fits their intent.

2. **Fear of Discomfort**

   Living intentionally means saying no to people, habits, distractions. That's uncomfortable. And humans hate discomfort.

3. Borrowed Intent

We inherit other people's dreams: parents' expectations, society's definition of success, and social media's flex culture. We end up living someone else's life while ignoring our own. And yes, I'll have to flex on social media too — not because I suddenly love posing with hashtags, but because marketing demands it. The difference is intent: not chasing likes, but reaching the readers this book is meant for.

The Cost of Unintentional Living

Unintentional living looks harmless until years pass. Then regret sets in.

- The career you never wanted but stuck with because it "made sense."
- The relationship you stayed in because "what will people say?"
- The habits you never broke because comfort felt safer than change.

Living unintentionally is like being in a car on cruise control — it feels smooth until you realise you're headed toward a cliff.

Story: The Wake-Up Call

A friend of mine had a "perfect life": stable job, nice car, family approval. But every day, he woke up with heaviness. One day, he admitted: "I don't even know why I'm doing all this." That's the silent scream of unintentional living. Outward success, inward emptiness.

He eventually left the job, downsized his lifestyle, and started something aligned with his real intent. Was it easy? No. Was it worth it? Absolutely.

The Pillars of Living Intentionally

1. **Clarity of Intent**

   You can't live intentionally if you don't know what you want. Write it down. Be brutally honest. Don't hide behind "respectability."

2. **Boundaries**

   Living intentionally means protecting your energy. Say no more often. Cut out people and habits that don't align.

3. **Time Awareness**

   How you spend your time is how you spend your life. Audit your days. Do they reflect your intent?

4. **Courage**

   Intentional living often offends people. They'll say you've changed, you're selfish, you're crazy. Courage is choosing your intent over their comfort.

The Minimalism Myth

Many people confuse intentional living with minimalism. Throwing out clothes, deleting apps, living in a white-painted room. That may help some people, but intentional living isn't about owning less — it's about owning what matters. For some, that's ten outfits. For others, that's fifty. Intent decides, not Instagram trends.

Intentional Relationships

Living intentionally reshapes how you connect with people.

- You stop entertaining "half-friends" who drain energy.
- You stop dating for validation and start choosing partners aligned with your future.
- You stop pretending to care about things that don't matter to you.

Suddenly, your circle shrinks. But it also deepens. That's the price — and the reward — of intentional living.

Intentional Work

The same applies to daily habits. Intentional living doesn't always mean a dramatic lifestyle overhaul. Sometimes it means doing the same routine with a clearer purpose — cooking not just to eat, but to care for yourself; exercising not to impress, but to stay alive longer. That clarity changes everything.

The Role of Logic and Instinct

- Logic helps you test if your "intentional" choices are sustainable.
- Instinct helps you sense when you're drifting off track.
- Together, they keep your intent from turning into either fantasy or burnout.

My Own Shift

For years, I chased things because they looked shiny. Jobs, opportunities, people. My intent wasn't clear — it was borrowed. Only when I started asking, *"What do I actually want?"* did life shift. I didn't suddenly become perfect. I still waste time. I still scroll reels. But I do it consciously now, not out of habit. That's the difference. And by the way, I'm still working on it — just in case you thought I turned into some Zen monk while writing this book. Not going to lie.

Living Intentionally Is Not Easy

Let's Be Real: intentional living doesn't always look glamorous. It often feels like saying no when everyone else is saying yes. It's trading quick dopamine for slow progress. It's awkward, clumsy, even boring at times. But growth rarely comes dressed in comfort — it usually shows up wearing discomfort.

Pause and Reflect

- Where in your life are you living on autopilot?
- What's one small choice today you can make with clear intent?

- Who drains your energy most — and why are you still entertaining them?
- If your life ended tomorrow, would the last year reflect your intent?

Epilogue
Think Beyond

So here we are. After all the talk about logic, instinct, and intent, the million-dollar question remains: Now what?

Books often end with neat answers, as if life were a tidy checklist. But let's be real — life doesn't care about your checklists. It will throw you surprises, heartbreaks, plot twists, and random detours. Some days, logic will save you. Some days, instinct will. Some days, intent will carry you when everything else fails. And some days, nothing will work, and you'll just sit there eating chips, wondering what the hell went wrong. That's life.

The point isn't perfection. The point is awareness. If you walk away from this book with one thing, let it be this: stop living on autopilot. Pause. Ask why. check if your logic, instinct, and intent are shaking hands or fighting in a corner. That small awareness can change everything.

The Real "Think Beyond"

The title of this book isn't about rejecting reason. It's about going beyond it. Logic is amazing but limited. Instinct is sharp but messy. Intent is powerful but slippery. Together, they don't give certainty — they give clarity. And clarity is enough.

Because here's the truth: you will make mistakes. You will trust the wrong people, misread your gut, chase the wrong goals. But if you live with awareness, those mistakes won't break you. They'll teach you. And that's what "Think Beyond" really means — using logic, instinct, and intent not as crutches, but as companions.

A Personal Note

Writing this book wasn't easy. Not because of the words—those eventually showed up — but because it forced me to confront myself. I had to admit where I had been dishonest with my intent. Where I had ignored my instinct. Where I had worshipped logic and still failed. In many ways, this book is less about teaching you and more about documenting my own messy experiments with being human.

And yes — let me say this before anyone else does: I am human, imperfect, and I make plenty of mistakes. I will continue to make them. Forever. So don't bother pointing out: "Oh, but you wrote a book, shouldn't you be perfect?" No, I shouldn't. This book isn't a certificate of holiness. It's just one flawed human thinking out loud. If you wanted flawless wisdom, maybe ask Google Maps or your grandma's WhatsApp group.

What Comes Next

Don't expect a transformation overnight. Start small. check your intent in one daily action. Listen to your instinct once a day. Use logic to double-check your choices. Over time, these tiny alignments will build a life that feels yours.

And when you mess up? Smile. Say, "Okay, I'm still human." Then try again. That's all any of us can do.

Final Thought

To Think Beyond is to refuse autopilot.

To Think Beyond is to live awake.

To Think Beyond is to choose clarity over convenience, honesty over approval, alignment over chaos.

Acknowledgments

Books are never written alone. Yes, the typing is often solitary, but the energy, the influence, the encouragement — that's collective.

First, to my parents — your quiet sacrifices, your faith, and your lessons built the foundation of everything here. You may never have used words like "logic, instinct, and intent," but you lived them, and I learned by watching.

To the readers — whether you're here because you love books, or because you got tricked by the title, or because someone shoved this into your hands — thank you. The fact that you gave me your time, the most precious currency we all have, means more than anything.

Closing Note

Life won't always reward you for being logical.

It won't always praise you for trusting instinct.

And it won't always celebrate your intent.

But if you live with awareness, you'll reward yourself with peace — and that's better than applause.

So, here's my wish for you: may your logic guide you, may your instinct protect you, and may your intent free you.

And whenever life tempts you to shrink, settle, or surrender — may you always remember to Think Beyond.

And before you close this book, let me admit something—

I believe I am imperfect, and always will be.

But that's exactly what makes me human.

Because imperfection isn't failure — it's the space where growth happens.

It's what keeps us curious, humble, and real.

Everyone makes mistakes. Everyone misjudges, overthinks, or forgets their own lessons — including me.

We're all incomplete in our own ways, constantly learning how to balance logic, instinct, and intent.

No one ever becomes "finished." And maybe we're not supposed to.

So may this book guide you — and me — whenever we lose our way.

Because I'm not done learning. I'm not done failing.

I'm not done figuring out who I am.

And neither are you.

Think beyond your fears.

Think beyond your mistakes.

Think beyond the illusion of perfection.

Because peace isn't found in getting everything right — it's found in staying honest through everything wrong.

And if these words ever echo back to you, let them remind you that you were never meant to be flawless — only aware, awake, and alive.

— ***Rishabh Choure***

Still learning. Still imperfect.

Still thinking beyond.

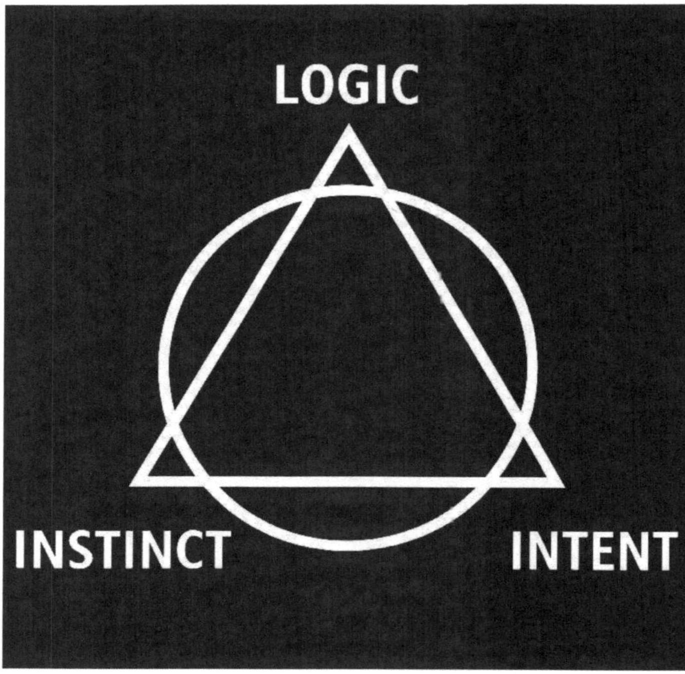
LOGIC
INSTINCT
INTENT

9 789374 263532

Printed at Repro India Ltd.